Getting Back on Your Feet
After Losing a Loved One

By Danny Bailey
Illustrated by Hannah Whyman-Naveh

Getting Back on Your Feet

After losing a loved one

Foreword

Danny was eating his breakfast one morning, when he said "Mum, I feel happy." "That's great!" I replied. "No," he said, "you don't understand, I really do feel happy and I thought I never would again after Dad died." This was quickly followed by "Oh no! What about all the other children that have lost someone special, who don't know that they will be happy again? I have to tell them that they will be OK!"
And so, the book began....

Nicky Bailey

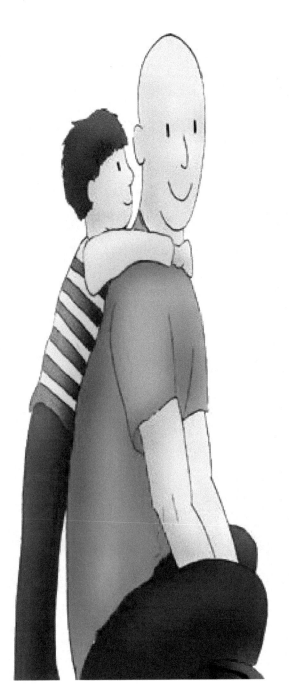

About The Author

Hi, I'm Danny Bailey and I'm eight years old. My dad died suddenly with no warning when I was five and three quarter years old, he had something wrong with his heart and it caused Sudden Arrhythmic Death Syndrome. To me he was the best dad in the world, and we spent a lot of time playing and doing things together so it was the worst time of my life. When it happened nothing felt right anymore and I thought I would never be happy again, but I am happy, so I want to tell you some of the things that helped me and I hope that they will help you to be happy again too.

When it First Happened

Me and my mum stayed at my granny and grandad's house for two weeks after it happened, and my aunt took two weeks off work to spend time with me. Family and friends came to see us there too to make sure we were ok. While we were there somebody suggested that we rang a local charity who help bereaved children, so my granny rang them. They helped me and my mum a lot so I will tell you more about them later.

Me and My Mum

My mum is very sad about losing my dad too, so we do a lot of things together to remember him. On his birthday we always take a small cake (My dad LOVED cake!) and a candle to his spot in the churchyard and we light the candle, say "Happy birthday" and eat the cake. We buy him a small present to leave on his spot too. We've bought things like a tiny little guitar and a tiny little laptop because those were his favourite things. We buy or make things for him at Christmas too and on Christmas Eve we go to the Christingle at the church and they give us glow sticks and we put those on Dad's spot too. It can be sad, but it makes me feel happy to sort of keep him close and make him part of special days.

I talk to my mum a lot about Dad because she says it's good to get my feelings out and not keep them inside of me and I think that's true, because I always feel better after we have talked. We talk about the things we miss about him and remember things that we did together and the funny things that he used to do. We have lots of cuddles while we talk and that helps a lot. Sometimes I cry and sometimes I don't and either of those is ok. Sometimes me and my mum both cry together and that's fine too.

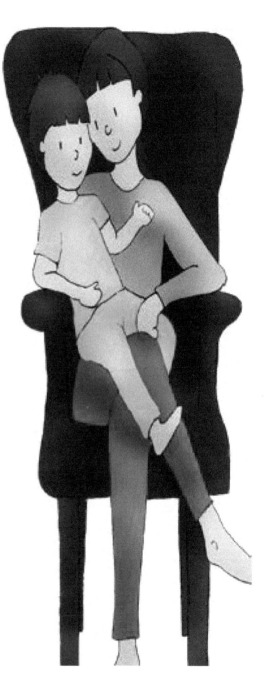

One Step at a Time

I think the most important thing for me was to just take things slowly and take one step at a time. When it first happened, most people wanted me to get back into a normal routine as soon as possible but that wasn't easy for me. I struggled with a lot of things especially if I had to do them without my mum, like eating in the school canteen and going on school trips or swimming with the school. I didn't feel like I could go anywhere unless she was with me.

My mum spoke to my school, family and friends and she told them that I was only going to do things when I felt ready and comfortable to do them and she didn't let anyone make me do anything that I wasn't ready for and that helped a lot. I went home for lunch for about six months before I felt ready to join in with the other children at lunchtimes. My head teacher at school let my mum come on school trips and on swimming lessons as a parent helper so I didn't have to miss out and after a while she arranged a trip to the beach in our village to help me take the next step of doing a trip without her and without having to be too far away from her and I actually enjoyed it.

I have also been to see a pantomime in the next town without her and that was great too. I'm now moving on to places a bit further away. So, when you feel like you're ready to try to take another step forward let your family and teachers know so that they can help you. If you need something or somebody to help you take the next step, tell somebody because they can usually help and every time you take a step forward you feel so much better and much more confident. Each time I achieved something I knew that I was going to get better.

Children's Bereavement Charities

The first thing that our local bereavement charity did was they sent a lovely lady out to see me at home. We talked about all sorts of things that were happening to me because things had changed so much. She brought a big box of crafts round too. She came to my house and my school a few times and she taught me lots of different ways to sort out things that I was struggling with. We did a lot of that with crafts, like a friendly spider. It had a body made from a wool pom-pom and the legs were made from pipe cleaners. Each leg was a different colour, and each colour represented somebody that was still here and that loved me and that was to help me to remember that although my dad is gone I'm not alone and I still have lots of other people that love me and look after me. I made a bracelet with my mum with different

 coloured wool plaited together so that I could wear it wherever I was and remember the people that I still have around me in the same way.

I worried about a lot of things; the biggest worry was that my mum might die too. I didn't understand why my dad died because he was healthy so I thought it could happen to her too. My bereavement worker gave me a little box and some stickers to decorate it and we made a worry box. I had to write my worries down with reasons why I don't need to worry so much about them, like my mum is still quite young and looks after herself so there is no reason for her to die early like my dad.

The bereavement charity invited us to an activity day with other children that had lost somebody special to them and that was good because I didn't know anyone else that it had happened to and I felt very different from all my friends. While we were there we made memory jars, it was brilliant fun. They gave us little jars, coloured chalk and lots of salt. We coloured the salt by rubbing the chalk over it and then we put a layer of each colour into the jar. Each colour represented a special memory of our special person and we wrote those memories on a tag that we tied to the top of our jar.

At the end of the activity day we all wrote down a message to our special person and tied it to a balloon filled with helium. We all went outside and let them go together to send our messages to our loved ones. Some people prefer to blow bubbles because they are better for the environment.

They gave me some books, the best one was called "Muddles, Puddles and Sunshine". It was very helpful, and I still use it sometimes. It explained a lot about different things that I was going through and there were spaces for me to write down how I felt about those things and there were crafts and activities in it to help me too. One of the ideas in it was a first aid box (I call it the "idea ambulance"). I got a box and lots of pieces of paper and on each bit of paper I wrote something down that might help me to feel better when I was sad like 'ring a friend', 'play football', 'cuddle someone I love', 'listen to music' etc etc etc. If I needed to, I could go to my first aid box, reach in and pull out something that might help me. I used this book a lot when I felt sad and when I read it now, I can see that I am finding everything much easier than I did when I first got it.

Techniques

I was worried that I might forget about my dad one day, so I wrote my favourite memories down and put them all in a jar to help me remember them. So now if I want to think about him, I can go to my jar and pull out a happy memory that will make me feel better.

One of the biggest things that has helped me is the fundraising for the bereavement charity that I have done with my mum to say thank you for all of their help and to help others that are going through the same thing. It took us a while before we felt ready to do this, but it helped us a lot and we still do as much as we can for them.

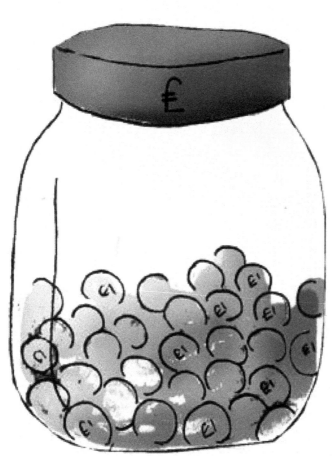

Resources

The charity also gave me things to help with my sadness and worries. They gave me a stress ball that I could squeeze as hard as I could to get my feelings out if I felt angry or frustrated. They also gave me a worry eater which is a soft toy with a zip for a mouth. You write down your worries on a piece of paper and put it in his mouth and zip it up and let it take care of that worry for you so that you don't have to worry about it. They gave me some books

too, I've already mentioned "Muddles, Puddles and Sunshine" but another book that I found very helpful was "Water Bugs and Dragonflies". I didn't really understand death when it happened, but this book helped me to look at it in a different way and really made me feel more comfortable about it all.

Days Out

The charity taught me lots of different ways to cope with different feelings, but they taught me and my mum how to be happy again too. We tried going to fun places, but we didn't enjoy them in the same way that we used to, and it didn't feel right to be happy when Dad wasn't with us. They arranged for us to go on a fun day at a local Royal Air Force (RAF) base eleven months after it happened. We had a brilliant time, and I didn't notice it at the time but a few months later my mum said that she thought that was the day when we learnt to enjoy ourselves again and I think she was right. You might not feel like you can enjoy yourself for quite a while, but it is possible, you can do it.

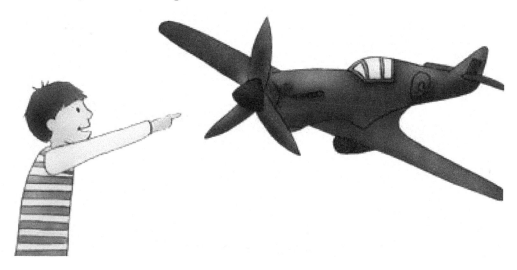

The activity day that they invited me to wasn't just making crafts, we went outside on an assault course too. It was great fun and gave me a bit of a boost in my confidence about going out and doing fun things.

The other day out that they gave us was a trip to our local pantomime. I can understand why they chose that because it was so funny and we laughed and laughed all through it. I would definitely recommend doing things like these when you feel up to it because I felt like I was able to just forget everything that had happened to me and just have fun like I used to and it felt good.

God

Some people believe in God, some don't. I do, and I used to blame him for taking my dad away from me but now sometimes I think that maybe he had a reason for taking him. I feel like he is happy in heaven and it makes me happy to think that.

Advice

The most important piece of advice is to talk about it often. It feels good to get all of your feelings out of your head and the person you are talking to can often help with your worries.

Sometimes when everything feels bad it can help to think about positive things. It might be the family and friends or a pet that you still have around you or the place that you live in or the school that you go to, anything that makes you feel happy or lucky to have.

Have lots of hugs, remember you still have people that love you and it helps if you let them look after you.

A Final Word From Danny

When it happened, I felt absolutely terrible and I felt like it was partly my fault because I wasn't there with him when it happened, but now, looking back, I realise that it wasn't my fault because if something like that happens, whatever you do, don't blame yourself because if the ambulance people couldn't do anything then neither could you. And most importantly remember that you will feel better over time even if you don't believe it now, things will get easier. Now, I know you love them so so much because so did I but I am feeling better about it. If you do feel yourself starting to cry as I do while I'm writing this, it's alright, it's even good for you and as I've said you will feel better one day. Just keep telling yourself that because you will, just one day.

Though I will never forget my dad, or stop loving him, I know I can have a good future ahead of me and so can you. You are a good person and it wasn't your fault, and know that if you do want to cry, it's alright.

I am learning to be happy again and enjoy my life but I am still keeping my dad as close as I can as a wonderful memory.

Questions and Answers

Q. Did you feel like you would never feel happy again?
A. Yes, I did feel like that.

Q. Do you still feel that way now almost three years later?
A. No. I do know that I still will be sad from time to time but I know that I can be happy too.

Q. Did you ever feel angry or confused?
A. Yes, I felt all kinds of different feelings but that's ok because it's good to get all your feelings out and not keep them inside.

Q. Does talking about it help?
A. Yes. Sometimes it can be very hard to talk about but if you talk to somebody that you love and trust it helps a lot.

CPSIA information can be obtained
at www.ICGtesting.com
Printed in the USA
LVHW071709040221
678389LV00018B/2824

9 781527 283732